I DON[illegible]

POEMS in Search of Reason

♦♦♦♦♦♦♦♦

Roger Huisinga

Mayhaven Publishing

P O Box 557
Mahomet, IL 61853
USA

Cover Design by Doris R. Wenzel

Library of Congress Control Number: 2005923129
First Edition—First Printing 2005
1 2 3 4 5 6 7 8 9 10

ISBN 1932278-12-5

Dedicated to the one who taught me:
One determined man can change the world.

A Note from the Editor

Poetry may be the most honest literature, generally depicting an author's perception at the very moment of writing. The author's words need not reflect earlier perceptions or those that may follow, but they place onto paper a moment in time to be considered and reconsidered. Roger Huisinga writes of his world, driven by his own determined curiosity.

—Doris Wenzel, Mayhaven Publishing

I DON'T KNOW JACK

I've been living this long and I don't know jack.
When I think I'm smart, life gives me a smack.
I've written things down about the lessons I've learned,
about the many times that I've been burned,
about the costly prices I have paid,
about the times I've fallen and the errors I've made.
I guess mostly what I'm trying to do
is to help you through a situation or two.
If I can light your way with what I've seen
you might run the same path a little more clean.
So these lines aren't written so much for me
but with you in mind, quite honestly.
As you read these words I hope they're food
for an inquisitive, positive attitude.
And if from my experience you can gain,
you'll have one less thing to cause you pain.

ANSWERS

We stumble through life looking for answers.
I wonder, do we look like blind-folded dancers?
As we search the hills, the dales, the cracks
how do we lift this weight from our backs?
Why am I here at this place and time?
Why does one man choose work, one man choose crime?
When there is no path, with machetes we carve one.
We must blaze a trail in order to find one.
The answers in life are hidden in the journey
To find them we must take the journey.
Curiosity almost killed the cat.
The race of man is much like that.
Take the journey and along the way
you may find the answers one day.

LET'S FLY

As a child I dreamed that I could fly.
I thought about it often. I really don't know why.
When the wind came up, I'd just raise my arms
and she'd lift me up with all her charms.
High up I'd go and soon could see
the uppermost apple on the apple tree.
I'd glide on by, above our house,
smile on my face, quiet as a mouse.
Then I'd swoop down by the barn and scare the cows
and rise again over tractors and plows.
I could feel the wind blowing through my hair.
I could soar like an eagle without a care.
It's true I was just a little tyke,
but I saw what the Good Lord's view was like.
Much later, when I climbed the ladder's stair,
it looked exactly like it did when I flew up there.

THE LADDER

I was four years old and ornery as hell.
Mom sent me outside to play for a spell.

I liked to climb trees and things like that.
I could climb to the top just like a cat.

That day I was messing around by the old grain bin.
It was locked up tight so I couldn't get in.

Above me a bird was starting to chatter
so I looked up and I saw this ladder.

At four years old I was just a pup
so for the bottom of the ladder I had to jump up.

I couldn't reach it on the first try
but I kept trying. I don't know why.

I climbed that ladder to the top.
When I got up there I didn't want to stop.

There was another ladder up there, you see,
so it was up to the peak of the bin for me.

I got up there and looked around.
It was pretty cool—thirty feet off the ground.

I sat on the cap and looked at our farm
I didn’t think there was any harm.

I could see our dog way down by the house.
He was barking at the door like he’d seen a mouse.

Out the door to check on me came my mom.
When she saw me up there she wasn’t too calm.

She climbed the ladder, too, to visit with me.
Then we climbed down together—kind of slowly.

Over the years she has told me many times
that it wasn’t one of her favorite climbs.

Later that night she told my dad
about all the great fun we had.

PICK UP A BOOK

Reading book after book when I was a child,
I let my imagination run wild.
Reading of people and places so far away,
many times I felt like I was there that day.
At Gettysburg I heard Abe's address,
half the crowd happy, half in distress.
With The Swamp Fox I crouched down in the fog
waiting and hiding behind a big log.
With Columbus I crossed the ocean wide
and wondered if there really was another side.
With courage I fought at The Alamo.
Would morning come? I did not know.
With Jackie I rode downtown with Jack.
Did anyone know he'd never be back?
With Martin I walked down in "Alabam."
We had a point to make. We gave a damn!
Each place exciting, each one unique,
each found in a book, if you'll take a peak.
There's an incredible life for which you'll yearn
so please pick up a book. There's much to learn.

CHORE TIME

I was still pretty young and a strong-minded boy.
I didn’t mind work but I’d rather play with a toy.
’Middle of the depression when times were rough,
my dad worked hard and folks said he was tough.
We had several cows we had to milk every day.
I was learning to help but still mostly got in the way.
Going into town was a once-a-month treat.
We’d get cleaned up from our head to our feet.
Before we could go, we would tend to the cattle
and getting me to help was kind of a battle.
But this Saturday Dad said we might go to town
but before we could go I had to drive the cattle down,
get them into the barn, and start with the milking.
I messed around too long, my job I was bilking.
Before I got started Dad appeared down the lane,
the look on his face was perfectly plain.
He helped me drive in the cattle and do all the chores,
but when he came inside he closed up the doors.
“I guess this week we won’t go to town,”
Dad told my mother with an unhappy frown.
I felt pretty bad because it was me
that screwed up our trip to the city.
You can bet the next Saturday the chores were done
and we went into town and had us some fun.

JUST HORSING AROUND

Our family was close, that's for sure.
Loving and giving is how they were.
On Sunday, after church, they'd always meet
for the big dinner that Grandma made to eat.
After dinner the grandkids went out to play,
and we hitched up the cart to the pony one day.
It was a beautiful afternoon with lots of sun,
and we let the pony get out and run.
Four young kids and a pony in a make-believe race.
It wasn't exactly the picture of grace.
We were having so much fun, our heads in the breeze,
we didn't really notice the upcoming trees.
The horse went through them. The cart did not,
and four kids went flying out like a shot.
It was Joe and Jim and Beulah and Dorr.
Young Beulah got hurt the worst of the four.
There was a nasty crack on the side of her head,
but in town was a sawbones called Dr. Bumstead.
My uncles scooped her up and headed for the Doc
to get her sewed up—they were racing the clock.
The Doc stitched her up and gave the o.k.
So they brought her home safely later that day.
The rest of us found out fast enough
that horsing around can get pretty rough.

—Story suggested by Joe Huisinga

MAMA KNEW BEST

We lived up north when I was a kid.
Mama told me to wear my hat, but that's not what I did.
As I walked around the corner I took it off
even though she warned me I'd get a cough.
I had long, flowing hair with a little bend
and I liked the way it looked blowing loose in the wind.
Mother had good advice, that much is true,
but I didn't always do what she told me to do.
I always ditched my hat on the way to school,
but one winter day it got real cool.
I had to walk quite a ways to get back home,
and my ears were freezing on the side of my dome.
I walked a little faster to get out of the cold
and when I hit the front door I wasn't so bold.
It seems my ears were frozen solid out on the tips.
Mama gave me hot chocolate and I took a few sips.
She said, "I thought I told you to wear your hat.
You don't have nine lives. You're not a cat.
You don't mess around with wind and weather.
It'll blow a girl like you around like a feather."
The very next day my ears were black,
a little frostbite made me glad I had my hat back.
I had put Mama's good advice to the test
and in the end Mama knew best.

AUNT MABEL

I went with Aunt Mabel down to the bank.
We needed bread and sugar and gas in our tank.

Once we had gotten our money and walked away
we were doing our errands and starting our day.

But down at the store, while paying the clerk,
my aunt discovered a strange little quirk.

She had ten more dollars than she should have had
I said, "Goodie," but my aunt said, "this is bad."

I said, "Can't we keep it?" and she said, "No."
Back to the bank we were destined to go.

My aunt never thought of keeping that money.
She said, "That just wouldn't be right now, honey."

Kids gain their values from what they see.
I sometimes wonder who is watching me.

If your barometer for what is wrong and right
hinges on whether you're out of sight,

there might be a problem beginning there
and inevitably it's a problem you're going to share.

Because your kids are sharp and they learn fast, too,
you can bet they're going to copy you.

Drinking or smoking or taking drugs,
cussing or chewing or fighting with thugs,

whatever the habit you just can't shake,
that's probably the same road your kids will take.

"Do what I say and not what I do,"
are words that will end up burning you.

We all make mistakes. That's how we live.
If we screw up, ask them to forgive.

But let's not make screwing up the rule.
There are little ones watching you just can't fool.

SMOKING

It was 1969 and I was eight years old.
I was mad at my dad if the truth be told.

So I got a pack of Marlboros out of the old red truck.
I was going to start smoking—thought I'd try my luck.

So I went out to the orchard, pack in hand
and I lit one up and thought I looked grand.

If Dad could smoke all day, then I could smoke one.
I smoked one more before I was done.

You see my Grandpa had cancer and was in a little pain.
Everyday he'd come out and walk around the lane.

When he got done walking he came up to me,
said, "Boy I seen you smoking up there in that tree."

That's all he said and just walked inside.
He left me hanging without an ounce of pride.

He didn’t say good, he didn’t say bad,
he never gave an opinion of what he thought of this lad.

I guess he just figured I already knew
that smoking in the orchard wasn’t the thing to do.

I’ve never felt worse than I did that day.
I imagine that’s why he handled it that way.

From that day on it was understood
that smoking anymore wouldn’t be any good.

He never told my mom, he never told my dad
he never again mentioned the little talk we had.

Grandpa passed away later that year.
My family and I shed many a tear.

But I figure Grandpa knew before he passed away
he had taught me how to think for myself that day.

TEACHER'S VOICES IN MY EAR

Teach people to survive out on their own.
At first they'll resist and moan and groan.

But teach them to cipher and speak and think
and they'll always find ways to eat and drink.

Most people know exactly what they want.
They just won't give up anything to get it, to be up front.

If the teacher hasn't taught until the student has learned
sometimes the textbooks need to be burned.

If people don't change something along the way
they'll end up where they are going someday.

Don't think everyone knows what you know
just because you told them once. Most people learn slow.

I just want to remind you the world's not going to end
if you've done something wrong, just don't do it again.

If you are 'master of your fate' and 'captain of your soul'
focus on positive thoughts and you will reach your goal.

The negative effect of stinking thinking
can sometimes equal drugs and drinking.

If you can find some quiet time in which to think
you can mostly brush off all the stink.

Do you imagine that a skunk knows that he smells?
Who you hang out with should ring some bells.

If you keep yourself focused on just your goals
you won't see that the road has many potholes.

DO IT RIGHT

We were farmers, then, as we are today.
Dad hired a new farm hand one spring day.

He was a kid from town and a little green
still a teenager and his boots were clean.

He didn't know much about working a farm
but he could tell a joke with a country charm.

Grandpa brought out a tractor from the shed
told the kid to go out and make a seed bed.

So he hopped on the tractor and off he went.
He was excited to go where he'd been sent.

After a few minutes he came walking back
said that old tractor had stopped in its track.

He was tooling along disking up grass
and that old tractor had run out of gas.

Grandpa met him at the tank with a red gas can.
It seemed like this was part of his plan.

Grandpa pulled the dejected kid aside
and as he said these words his smile grew wide,

"Boy, I guess next time you'll check that tank."
The kid agreed although his face looked blank.

He learned a good lesson on his very first day.
"When you work here, kid, you do it the right way."

That kid worked a few years and then moved on,
but many years after he'd been gone

he passed that story on to me
and he remembered my grandpa affectionately.

THE DRIVING LESSON

The mailbox sat down the road in the olden days.
To pick up our letters we'd have to walk a ways.

I'd just turned sixteen and I could drive the car
and that mile walk was way too far.

So I hopped in the car and for the mail I went.
It was a pretty nice car, not a scratch or dent.

I threw the mail on the seat and was on my way back
when I saw a letter with my name in the stack.

I opened that letter without a hitch
and as I read it, I drove right into the ditch.

I wasn't hurt but I wrecked the car pretty good.
My neighbor came along and did what he could.

He drove me to the house and said I'd be in trouble
that when my dad found out, he'd bust my bubble.

We drove right up to the house and he let me out
and as he drove away I began to pout.

I told dad my story and when I was done confessin'
He smiled and said, "I guess that was a good lesson."

His reaction really surprised me that day.
I never figured he would handle it that way.

Sometimes it's not so much what you do
but what the experience teaches you.

My dad knew that and now so do I.
Things rarely go perfect no matter how hard you try.

I remember it clearly though it's been fifty years.
Daddy reinforced the lesson and wiped away the tears.

THE STUD BARN

Grandpa was a breeder of Belgium horses.
They were huge and beautiful, one of nature's forces.
Families farmed with those horses back in the day
and those big horses ate lots of hay.
One day we heard Grandpa was to breed a mare
so we ran to the hayloft and we hid out there.
We were three youngsters, just curious boys.
We thought we could watch without making any noise.
We waited for hours or so it seemed.
When Grandpa finally showed up, our faces gleamed.
He put the young mare in the stall down there
then he brought in the stud to service the mare.
We were in the loft watching quiet as deer
when Grandpa stopped and yelled, "Boys come on down here!
If you boys want to watch, here's the front row,
otherwise, to the house is where you should go."
By now this wasn't as fun anymore
so with sheepish grins, we ran out the door.
We'd been sneaking around, trying to have fun
but when Grandpa caught us, our fun was done.
We learned a pretty good lesson that day
sneaking around just doesn't pay.

—Story suggested by Joe Huisinga

CIVIC DUTY

I was born and raised near a small country town.
We didn't let little things get us down.
The country way smacked of self reliance.
We did the best we could with proud defiance.
Things were hard sometimes but never bad.
Folks didn't seem to miss what they never had.
We didn't have the safety net of a big city.
We didn't get caught up in useless self pity.
My father served on the conservation board.
He served our little town and he served the Lord.
He said, "You don't ever want to pass up an opportunity
to do something worthwhile for your community.
This town will live or die on our good work.
It's not a duty that you want to shirk.
Teaching and helping and giving a hand
means we're doing something that God had planned.
And if in this life that's all you do
the world will be better when you're through."

IMPERFECT PEOPLE

Sometimes in life it seems you're covered in layers.
You wonder if God even hears all your prayers.

But in these tough times, the measure of a man
is proving to God and the world that he 'can.'

They say the Lord won't give you more than you can handle
and this ain't the time to cover your candle.

You've got to make your way before the Lord gives you more.
He needs you to grow and change before you get your next chore.

So dig into this battle and give it your all
and when the Lord calls your number, answer the call.

The Lord uses people all the time who are weak,
folks with kinks in their armor and flaws they must tweak.

If imperfect people all just gave up
there would be no one around to fill the Lord's cup.

To go out in the world and do the Lord's deeds,
sometimes an ordinary man does *not* follow—*he leads.*

So just when you feel you're ready to break
please pick up the Good Book, be selfish, and 'take.'

Take all that you need to make your world right.
Take all that you need to rejoin the fight.

And I'll bet you, my friend, when you put it down
your face will have already lost its big frown.

Faith in action will cancel your great misery.
You must work to fulfill your great destiny.

Every common man, every unworthy sinner
must serve the Lord God to become a winner.

So next time you feel just about ready to cry
pick up the torch and give it a try.

A challenge is merely opportunity to grow.
If you don't accept it, you'll never know

just what the Lord can shape you to be.
I think he wants *you* to change history.

TEACHING WITH STORIES

The Lord taught with stories, it's sometimes said.
But what do they mean, I've asked as I've read.
I think the answers all become clear
when we trust in the spirit and we're willing to hear.
The Lord leads us here and then over there.
He wants us to think and he wants us to share.
The fact that His answers do require thought
means he wants us to use the brain that we've got.
Nothing in life is worse than free choice
or better perhaps, how should I use my voice?
Should I climb on a mountain shouting His praise?
Would I look like a man in a drug-induced craze?
All things are possible for those who believe.
When you read a passage, you may perceive
exactly what you need at that point in time.
For another it might be a mountain to climb.
The words become clear when you have a need.
For others they will germinate just like a seed.
And just when they're needed they'll grow up again
to give comfort to someone who needs it then.
The Bible provokes these words and this thought.
If folks never read it what chance have they got?

THE OPTIMIST

They called him the optimist and I know why.
He didn’t see limits, not even the sky.
A problem was just something he would resolve.
When there was a riddle, his mindset was to solve.
When everyone else had all but given in
he gave one more surge and went for the win.
In life there are people who seem destined to fail.
Mention failure to him and he wouldn’t turn his tail.
He’d just dig in harder and give you reasons why
you were just as deserving as the other guy.
Whatever the score, he always found a way
to encourage his teammates and raise their level of play.
In sports or in life, it didn’t matter.
We all knew he would climb the ladder.
Most times problems seem big at the start,
but they lose their size when you tear them apart.
Obstacles pop up like bumps in the road,
so get up off the couch in your humble abode
and tackle the problems as they arise.
They’ll disappear quickly, much to your surprise.
You get optimistic when you have success.
Without optimism you just have a mess.

"TO MY DARLING WIFE ON MOTHER'S DAY"

You mean so much to me I just had to say,
could you wash my shirt, could you scratch my back,
could you pick up the kids, could you fix that crack,
could you mow the yard and take out the trash,
could you fix me dinner so I can crash?
Could you scrub the floor and fix that light,
but don't work too hard, that wouldn't be right.
Did you know the dishes don't really shine?
Please don't wear that shirt; you know it's mine.
Could you fold those towels the way I like?
What do you mean there's no time to ride your bike?
Could you dress up for dinner and look real nice?
Could you make sure you listen to my advice?
And if we ever argue, when we're done
could you make sure to tell me that I've won?
And when you're done with these little things
could you stop and kiss that wedding ring.
I wonder, honey, can you take a joke
or is there someone you'd like to choke?
I say all these things just in jest
'cause you know what darling? "You're the best!"

—Love, Roger

ROSIE

He had an infectious laugh and a full head of hair.
What others thought, he mostly didn’t care.
When it came down to it, he was the one
who required that life be some kind of fun.
He had a love of planes and things that could fly.
To him, the limits of life just didn’t apply.
He’d go out of his way to say, “Hello,”
and mostly he left you with a warm friendly glow.
Somehow he seemed to avoid most of life’s worry,
and it was rare to find him in much of a hurry.
There was something about his way that brought a smile
and when you’d cross paths, he’d always visit awhile.
I guess he was misunderstood by some;
he lived life to the beat of a different drum.
Over all, around him, I’d say we had
a lot more good times than we ever had bad.
Sometimes it’s hard to make peace with the dead.
How do we tell them what’s locked in our head?
But with Rosie, I think we can rest assured
if we ever had problems right now they’re cured.
And what better thing can you say in the end,
“Come hell or high water, he was my friend.”

THE TRAIN

Here's a little story about my son Jim.
One summer day we were awful proud of him.
It was 1935 and he was nearly 10
and for the first time he got to work with the men.
It was threshing time in our neighborhood.
Later that night it was supposed to rain pretty good.
We were moving the thresher on up the line
to do the next fellow's and then do mine.
As he was crossing the railroad, the driver looked back.
His big steel wheel had pulled up the track.
We all knew this wasn't very good,
so we decided to do the only thing we could.
We sent Jim down the track with a big red flag,
a canteen of water, and some lunch in a bag.
We said, "No matter what, you've got to stop that train.
We've got to keep moving because it's going to rain.
All by himself, he just waited around.
After a couple hours he could hear the sound
of that big steam engine coming around the bend.
He had to get them stopped, or they'd meet their end.

In the middle of the track, he flagged back and forth.
The train was running fast and headed up north.
He worried this might turn out like a nasty dream
when finally he heard them backing down the steam.
He walked right up to the steaming engineer
who said, "What the hell are you doing here?"
Jim told them about the bad track ahead.
"Good thing, boy, we might have ended up dead."
They telegraphed a crew to come and fix that track
and the engineer gave Jim a pat on the back.
Even though he was scared, young Jim was brave.
That day, all by himself, there were lives to save.

DICK

We called him Foz, though his name was Dick.
His gate was slow but his wit was quick.
He was born and raised out on the farm
and he carried himself with a redneck charm.
He wore suspenders about every day;
wore a dirty old hat cocked the same old way.
He had loads of friends and loved to have fun.
He was always looking for a great deal on a gun.
He drove an old Dodge truck for a hundred years.
He loved Schlitz, not exactly the "king of beers."
He was our hunting buddy, but more than that—our friend
and our old buddy had it pretty tough toward the end.
But he came out to Deer Camp, anyway
to see his old buddies and spend the day.
We cross paths with thousands, befriend a special few.
We're proud to say Dick was part of our crew.
Some groups of friends have a special bond
that reaches from here to the great beyond.
So today we'll add our friend Dick's name
to our special Deer Camp Wall of Fame.

THE GIRL NEXT DOOR

The girl next door was learning ballet,
something we couldn't afford back in that day.
She was taking lessons in the back yard.
I tried not to look but it was just too hard.
I went over to the fence and looked through the crack
"Mind your own business!" the neighbor shot back.
I wasn't hurting nothing, just wanted to see,
but the neighbors didn't think too much of me.
We were poor, it's true, but we weren't bad.
Why would the neighbors make me feel so sad?
I guess they figured we were just no good.
Why they felt that way, I never understood.
Why do some people think they're better than others?
Aren't we all just sisters and brothers?
If they have more money does that make them better?
If she acts like that, I say forget her.
I decided that day, after crying for awhile,
that I wouldn't let them steal my smile.
I vowed that day I would always be
nicer to people who weren't like me.
And to this day when I look back
I don't believe there is a wrong side of the track.

FATHER OF SIX

He was the smartest dumb-ass I ever knew.
He was always, at least, one step ahead of you.
You could figure what most folks would do, more or less,
but with him, you didn't have the wildest guess.
He'd bet on anything and take either side
and you'd rarely beat him, no matter how hard you tried.
Most people you can read and be pretty close,
but mostly he'd give you just a big healthy dose
of the medicine to cure you from betting with him
because your margin for error was so very slim.
His friends all loved him, and some hated him too,
there was no telling the next thing he might do.
He was a trader at heart, always looking for a deal,
and if you didn't know value, he'd get things for a steal.
There were precious few people who could keep up with his wit,
and most of those who tried ended up regretting it.
He wasn't usually malicious, just having fun,
but if you ever crossed him, from then on you were done.
I've seen him run people out of a joint.
They felt so darned stupid just trying to make a point.
He spent too much time drinking, mostly cold beers,
and his lifestyle wore him down after so many years.
I didn't know him when he was young
but I've heard the stories until my ears have rung.
He was good in sports and a handsome lad.
People talked of the many talents he had.

His family farmed together and traded work.
There were so many youngsters, it drove the adults berserk.
So he was always surrounded with cousins and friends.
They told lots of stories with many different ends.
He ended up in college to play basketball,
but one year was enough. He heard the farm's call.
So he went back home and started to farm,
and married a lady with beauty and charm.
In less than a year they had a baby girl
and then, right away, gave it another whirl.
The total, in the end, stood at six
then his poor wife went in for the fix.
They had built a house and soon had to add on
with so many kids all the space was gone.
Farming was good, with grain and livestock.
He was building a fortune to take care of his flock.
He contracted diabetes and soon his kidneys failed.
He was full of poison and his face had paled.
He had to go for dialysis three times a week,
and after several years, he got the transplant he seeked.
But the disease kept advancing, almost blinding one eye,
then after an amputation he was a one-legged guy.
But he got a prosthesis and kept walking anyway.
He'd get up and strap it on every single day.
As the years moved on, his arteries got hard,
but his wit was still keen. You couldn't catch him off guard.

Until the day he had his first stroke
it took awhile to heal, but still he wasn't broke.
After that, he had trouble with his only good leg,
I guess one good leg was too much to beg.
So with two peg legs, he learned to walk again.
He'd hold on to his walker and sometimes give it a spin.
He couldn't drive a car, so he got a golf cart.
It was purple and white. It seemed to fit the old fart.
We called his ride the "Barney Mobile."
He got stuck sometimes. That was quite a bad deal.
He'd just have to sit there helpless and wait
until we went looking cause it was getting late.
All the locals would stop and visit by the road,
and he loved to watch the combines fill the next load.
He would sit and watch the neighbors farming for hours
That's what he'd been doing, if he hadn't lost his powers.
Eventually he had another stroke.
This would be enough to make most men choke.
He lost his left side, but battled on back
until he was walking again and back on track.
He was a calmer man now than in his younger days
He'd say, "What can I do about it anyway?"
He'd lost some of his fire and gained a little humor,
this easier-going man was kind of a late bloomer.
He loved to go to ballgames to see the last of his boys.
He'd stand and cheer them and make a little noise.
Without his children, I don't think he would have fought,
but he kept on battling for every second he got.

As time went by the disease struck again.
It was off to the doctor to lose another limb.
This time they took off half his left arm
and for awhile he was bitter, without the old charm.
But he fought his way back once again
even though his patience and his body grew thin.
Eventually he required too much care
so we moved him to the nursing home, down there.
We'd go to visit and his spirits were good,
but we really didn't go as often as we should.
He loved to spend time talking to his many grandkids
It was much different than the auctions, when he used to shout bids.
His life had come full circle, from youth to old age
He had a lot of wisdom, but his speech was no longer sage.
His memory still served him from years ago.
Bring up details of the past and he'd always know
the thing that no one else could remember,
but his calendar of life had reached December.
Out of four good limbs, now he had only one.
I suppose he longed for the days when he could run.
That old man fought hard, much harder than most
And I wouldn't be surprised if someday I saw his ghost
driving down the middle of the road in his "Barney Mobile,"
pedal to the metal and hand on the wheel.
Folks, as I tell you these words, I feel downright sad
because that tough son-of-a-gun, was my own, dear dad.

COOK

Our old buddy, Cook, won't be here this year
to join in the hunt for the biggest deer.
I'm pretty sure he'd like to be,
but you just can't overcome destiny.
Old Cook was a hunter, that's for sure.
Come wind or weather he'd endure.
When everyone said the chances were slim
he'd bring back the only deer with him.
From Michigan he came for a trophy buck.
He got lots of deer but had no particular luck
in finding the one that he dreamed about,
but from his last hunting trip he gave us a shout.
He'd finally found the buck he'd wanted,
the one for all his life he'd hunted.
He was happy as a lark when he made that call,
just checking in and telling us all.
For him that deer was a reason to live,
and until he got it, he just wouldn't give
in to the cancer burning away inside.
He just needed that one last ride.
The first day of camp I said to Ray,
"I kind of miss old Cook today."
He looked at me and said, "Me too."
And I' m sure it's no different for any of you.

THE MILLION DOLLAR PRIZE

There was an old farmer who had no heirs.
He farmed the ground and sold his wares.
He worked hard to make a dollar all his life.
Never found the one to call his wife.
The old farmer paid for his land over time.
He built the soil up with fertilizer and lime.
Little Timmy came in with a sheep’s disguise
and a detailed plan for the million dollar prize!
You see that’s about what the farm was worth
and to Timmy there’d be nothing better on earth.
So he got the old farmer to despise
the rest of his family with a pack of lies.
He’d say, “Old John did this” and “Jerry did that.”
He had the old man convinced in nothing flat.
So they marched to the lawyer’s and made a new will
And now little Timmy is the King of the Hill.
Thank you Timmy, from you we’ve learned
thou shalt not covet or you might get burned.
Not here on earth while you eat your spoils
but on the way to the land where the Good Lord toils.
For if in this world I’m a selfish king,
in the next I may not have a thing.

RED

His name was Johnny, but we called him Red.
Last week he was with us, though sick in bed.

But we'll remember him tall, remember him proud,
telling a joke and maybe laughing out loud.

He was a fine farmer and led a full life,
was tremendously proud of three sons and his wife.

He tried to teach his kids lessons, ones that would last,
ones that took advantage of his experience and his past.

Had some beautiful grandkids, loved them all,
would have given all he had, to see them grow tall.

"He's never been nothing but a good neighbor to me,"
said one of his buddies, speaking candidly.

Had leukemia for years but never complained,
wanted to set a good example for those who remained.

He lost his dad young, had to grow up fast.
When there was work to be done, he came in the house last.

Liked his tractors green, liked his Cubbies, too.
Talk bad about either and he'd argue with you.

He could figure out numbers real fast in his head.
"Dumb like a fox," it was sometimes said.

We'll remember his spirit, remember his fight,
that he'd stand behind you if he knew you were right.

And as we look back we remember good times.
We can't do him justice with silly old rhymes.

So on this day of honor for our friend Red,
let's remember him fondly, maybe bow our head.

Because the livestock is tended, the cattle have hay,
and he's going to meet his maker today.

'57 CHEVY

We just called him Timmy the Runt.
For a good black sheep, we didn't have to hunt.
In nineteen seventy-five he turned sixteen.
He acted nice, but he was really mean.
Showing off was what he did best.
He needed more attention than all the rest.
He came to our picnic one summer day
hot-rodding his car in the usual way.
He had a fifty-seven chevy, white and blue.
It was old enough to vote but looked like new.
He was out front spinning his tires around
when the car's transmission dropped to the ground.
His mom and dad were not filled with pride.
They finished eating and then towed his ride.
Of course Timmy didn't think he did anything wrong.
Blaming someone else was his usual song.
"Poetic justice" is what the people all said.
I'll remember that day until I'm dead.

THE MEETING

Timmy the Runt was at it again.
His actions were always veiled so thin.
I'm not here to judge, just to tell.
When your motives are bad, things don't go so well.
He was off to a meeting, or so he said,
but he ended up in the wrong girl's bed.
His neighbor happened by and caught him there
with unbuttoned clothes and tousled hair.
There ain't no secrets in a country town.
What goes up most generally comes down.
Where will it land is what we wonder.
Will it land real soft or with a clap of thunder?
Little Timmy decided to cut the affair off quick.
His neighbor kept quiet, though it made him sick.
He gave little Timmy one more try
to prove he wasn't such a useless guy.
I hope Little Timmy can find his way
before he lines up for judgment day.

THE GREAT CHEAP SHOT

We had a fishing buddy we called Big Joe.
How he got so big, I'll never know.

Every year in late summer we'd load up the trucks,
hook up the boat and head for the land of the bucks.

We made sure we had good tackle and plenty of beer.
We put a driver up front and played cards in the rear.

Up north we had a cabin next to Lake Birch.
We'd drop the boat in the water and begin our search.

To find the biggest bass is to what we aspired.
Fishing all day makes a fellow pretty tired.

Big Joe had quite a reputation up there.
When he stepped on the dock it creaked in despair.

He'd throw one unlucky guy in the water every year,
laugh a little while, and then throw them a beer.

This year Joe said it was my turn to swim.
On that little ramp there was no getting around him.

He headed down the ramp with a mighty chuckle.
Said, "You've had it now!" and tugged at his buckle

I smiled as he headed down my way.
I guess this was just going to be the day.

I figured getting wet would be no fun
so I lowered my head and made a run.

My old nickname was the Baby Bull,
and when I got to Joe I caught him full

beneath the arms and square in the chest
and I guess you all can guess the rest.

He began to teeter and then he fell.
He hit the water and stayed for a spell.

This time we threw Big Joe the beer
and the whole fishing camp was in good cheer.

Now Big Joe reminds me every chance he's got
about what he calls, "The Great Cheap Shot."

THE FUNNY PAPER

He was Wild Bill from Hickory Hill,
sometimes a saint and sometimes a pill.

He was a jolly man ’bout five feet six
and he was known for pulling funny tricks.

We were hauling corn out of his grain bin
when the auger we were using decided not to spin.

This made me mad, to say the least,
so on dirty words I had a feast.

As I was nearing the end of my tirade
Wild Bill pulled up and joined the parade.

He decided that a broken auger wouldn’t do
so we drove towards town for a part or two.

Inside the truck, up on the dash
was that day’s paper, our daily hash.

I picked that paper up to read
then I threw it down. I was just too tee’d.

Wild Bill grabbed the paper and gave his window a click
then threw it out the window into Goose Crick.

His sudden act caught me by surprise.
It was a brand new paper. This wasn't wise.

He said, "Screw that paper!" then took a breather.
"If it ain't good enough for you, it ain't good enough for me either."

Then he snorted at me with a mock serious look.
That was just about all it took.

We both started laughing as hard as we could.
Humor had worked when nothing else would.

Sometimes when you're going through some kind of strife
a sense of humor can brighten your life.

As I look back, I give credit to Wild Bill.
When serious won't help, humor often will.

THE GOOD HIRED HAND

Timmy the runt came from a good family
but he always wondered, "What's in it for me?"
His family had a farm near our home town
and Timmy was known for cutting people down
His family had a good hired man named John.
Timmy didn't know it because he was always gone
off to party or to an important meeting
he rarely gave John a nod or a greeting.
John was a good man with a great big heart
and Timmy took every chance to tear it apart.
He referred to John as their hired nigger.
It's no wonder Timmy never grew any bigger.
I think his growth was stunted by his little mind
so his body no doubt reacted in kind.
It was always John out working the fields.
It was always John who knew the yields.
Over the years John did all the work
while Timmy took the time to become a bigger jerk.
Finally one year old John retired.
The next three hired hands little Timmy fired.
Timmy the runt wasn't a very smart lad.
He didn't appreciate the easy life he'd had
But when John retired, he found out quick
it takes real work to make a farm click

FRIENDS

Sometimes when I don’t see my friends for awhile
they appear in my dreams wearing a smile.

Never mind where they are, or if they be dead,
they can pay me a visit when I lay down my head.

To see my friends, I don’t need a car.
Through my dreams I’ve traveled near and far.

And through these travels I’m so very glad
I can visit the best friends a man ever had.

INTELLIGENCE

The things in life we don't understand outnumber the things we do.
Sometimes it's real hard to explain what intelligence means to you.
Are you smart if you're good with numbers or if you read quite well?
Are you 'deep' if you know a theorom? How can you ever tell?
If you can work the daily puzzles, do you have things sorted out,
or do you think you're keener if you wield all kinds of clout?
Where do you look for wisdom in your daily life?
Where do you find your answers when you're facing lots of strife?
And are you leading your family with arrogance and might,
and do your troubles leave you wound a bit too tight?
What beacon do you follow? What shaped your thoughts until now?
You took the turns to get here. Did you eat the right brain chow?
In this age of heroes, do they deserve your admiration,
or are they just false idols of a lost generation?
Are you living life afraid of everything you'll lose?
If given a decision, how wisely will you choose?
In your little chess game, do you think you are the king?
There is an energy that binds us with every other living thing.
Sometimes the path we're taking doesn't have a light,
and when we're walking blindly, only faith can calm the fright.
So if you can't trust your compass and don't know which way to go,
and if for all your efforts you have nothing real to show,
there is something real important, dear friends, I'd like to share.
Open up your Bible. You'll find the answers there.

A CHILD'S NEEDS

All parents wonder, what does my child need,
surely a pat on the back for a good deed,
lots and lots of love we all must concede,
a kiss on the knee when it starts to bleed,
some of our time every day, guaranteed,
reasonable expectations for them to exceed,
many good books and a Bible to read,
chores to do or a garden to weed,
much good advice for them to heed,
a lesson or two about the perils of greed,
knowledge about life we can sow like a seed,
a bicycle to ride to learn about speed,
good food in the house on which they can feed,
patience and compassion when we get tee'd,
a good dog or cat—a friendly breed,
a few opportunities for them to lead?
Give them all these things, I beg and I plead,
then in this tough life your child will succeed.

LISTEN

What a teenager needs is someone who'll listen.
At this time in their life, this just can't be miss'n.
Someone who'll hold their tongue and not give advice,
absorb what they hear without thinking twice.
Someone to hear what they say and never budge,
hear the whole story and not be a judge.
Give them some time when they want to talk
maybe even suggest they take a little walk.
Sometimes they'll say nothing and that'll be fine,
or maybe they'll open up like a real gold mine.
It's very important that someone is there,
someone with compassion to show that they care.
It's not so important what words are said,
just a comfortable place where they know they can tread
and feel they fit in like a hand in a glove,
somewhere they know they can always feel love.
Too many people tell teenagers just what to do
before they listen enough to have a good view.
I wonder if people can remember back when
they were fifteen years old and didn't fit in,
back when they didn't know what the world was about,
back when they were just starting to figure things out.
So just open your ears and soon you will find
there is much you can learn from a teenager's mind.

PRINCIPLES

We start with a principle then add humanity,
the building blocks of religion—even Christianity.
We start with something that’s real and concrete,
but it’s rarely perfect when we take it to the street.
Most every rule has at least one exception,
something that tests the limits of our foggy perception.
We should stick with our principles, generally,
but that doesn’t dot every I and cross every T.
Although not really common, for those we need sense.
Is the grass always greener over the fence?
We live by the rules until the rules don’t apply
and then by the seat of our pants we must fly.
In these times when life goes somewhere brand new
we must lean on the Lord to pull us on through.
With his guidance, some sense will come to our head.
Without it we may go the wrong way instead.
So in water too deep or in air way too thin
rely on your maker to reel you back in.
In tough times he’ll carry you back to safe ground
if only you ask, his blessings are found.

CHOICES

I made a choice just the other day
and I wondered if I touched the world some way.

Does each choice we make change things forever
or is the mere thought a wild endeavor?

What if someday my choice is wrong
and another man's life doesn't last as long?

If I could go back and take a different road
would it lighten someone else's load?

The choices I make each and every day
are going to affect the world some way.

I think and wonder, did I choose right?
Did I choose well or out of spite?

Is there value in the things I do?
Am I helping others find value too?

Everyone we know and each person we meet
share the same, albeit, a different heartbeat.

What if the future of the world is up to me?
What if I'm the one to make others see?

Without me, good people just might not
ever find out about the chance they've got.

If I stayed silent or misbehaved
and because of me someone wasn't saved,

when I stand before God and he asks me why,
why I didn't make an effort to save that guy,

when he asks me that, what will I say?
"It wasn't my job to save the world that day?"

In the end are we worth very much
if others lives we never touch?

If we never share about our Lord
that's the kind of choice we can't afford.

My time on earth may not be long
so I'll try to make my choices strong,

and when I stand up on judgment day
I hope for someone, I've carved the way.

MOMENTUM

In sports there's an energy like no other,
a force that binds us to one another,

an entity so intangible we could never explain
how it lifts us up and changes the plane,

how it fills the stadium, the court, the field,
puts fans on edge with eyes and ears peeled.

Momentum is a power so extreme
you know you *have* to capture it for your team.

It makes you bullet-proof, like the man of steel,
but it can slide away like a slippery eel.

It resides on a pendulum way up in the air,
and to pull it your way takes work, not despair.

In the game it might take a wild ride.
At the buzzer we all want it on our side.

But how do you know just where it's found
when it's hovering invisible above the ground?

If you find a little, you can usually find more.
But when *they* have it, can you close the door?

Sometimes as it leaves, it makes your skin crawl.
Sometimes you can't find it. Is it there at all?

Yes and no is the obvious answer.
If it's yours, it's gold, if not, it's cancer.

When you start the game you're always looking
for a little momentum to get you cooking.

As the game wears on, you take great pride
if you can keep it tilting towards your side.

But when you feel it start to slip,
that's when you've got to let it rip!

You've got to run it down and get it back.
You can't give in. You must attack.

And if you really want to win
you have to snatch momentum back again.

YOUR BEST

There's just something about giving your best.
Don't be afraid to put yourself to the test.
There's just something about a satisfied smile
when you know you've gone the extra mile.
Some folks seem to think it's O.K.
If they decide to dog it one day.
You don't want failure to become a habit.
When opportunity knocks, you need to grab it.
Anything worth doing is worth doing wrong
because we can practice and do it right before long.
Some people say winning is the only thing,
but that's not the song I want to sing.
In whatever you do, do the best you can.
Getting better and better should be the plan.
If only your work can feel like play
you'll wake up healthy and happy most every day.
Make your life have value, no matter what your station.
Don't give in to bragging and exaggeration.

Defeat can help you grow and learn.
With experience you'll get your turn.
Set a goal and strive to make progress.
If it doesn't happen fast, don't feel you're worth less.
In the journey is where you'll find your best,
not at the top, peering out from the crest.
Each tiny step, each giant leap,
each time you looked at the mountain too steep,
each time the finish line seemed too far,
each time too early they raised the bar.
Looking back, these times you will remember,
the cold and desolate days of December
when your courage and will were very low
still you strapped on your boots and made them go.
These times you will value more than gold.
These are the stories your kids will be told
so they may also find their way
giving their best, like you, every day.

BASEBALL

Baseball is our pastime and most all people here embrace
the fact that we can play the game almost any place.

Baseball is our country's game, played throughout the years.
It is the source of many smiles and also many tears.

For whatever else it isn't, baseball is our game.
Where many of us falter is trying to place blame

for every little error and every small miscue,
for every strike we watched go by and for what we didn't do,

for every big mistake that's made, we should not make it seem
that if it weren't for that one guy, we'd have a better team.

A team is built of pieces, much like a family,
and if a piece doesn't fit too well, then maybe we should see

that if we all pitch in to help and give them some support
our team will be much better and so, too, will our sport.

The world won't end tomorrow if an umpire missed a call
and we shouldn't get in fights about things so very small.

Every man on every team can’t play his favorite spot
so if we don’t play where we want, let’s still give it all we’ve got.

In baseball and in life there are many things the same.
Not too many Baseball players will go on to see great fame.

Our success is in the journey, learning to stand tall
and learning to get back up quick when we take a fall.

In ten years we won’t remember the details of the game
but I’m sure we’ll look back fondly at our teammates just the same.

The best thing about baseball, what gives our smiles a gleam,
is that whatever we accomplished *we did it as a team.*

BASKETBALL

We always hustle, we play with pain,
we control the ball, we control the lane.

We always know where our ball's at,
we challenge our opponent right off the bat.

We play ball with our heads alert,
we always box out, we're tough as dirt.

We always know where our teammates are
"There's no "I" in team; I ain't no star."

We keep our dribble alive and protect the ball,
we are triple threats, we can do it all.

We make our opponent use their weakest hand,
we don't give up layups, that much we demand.

We can reverse, crossover, and go behind the back.
We'll take what they give us and then attack.

If we make a mistake we make it full speed,
"No whining or crying." That's our creed.

Before we act we always fake.
We get them leaning, then 'shake and bake'.

If their defense runs back with their heads down
we'll run up their backs and go to town.

We rebound and pivot, and make the outlet pass.
We'll keep the pressure on until they're out of gas.

We never let their best player control the game.
We'll deny the ball till you forget their name.

We play this game because it's fun
We're building our skills. We love to run.

We do all this work for pride, not wages,
we're the purple and gold. We are the Sages.

THE GAME OF LIFE

The game of life, such an intricate game.
Do we want lots of money? Do we want lots of fame?
What are the rules? I need to know.
Just give me a copy, I'm raring to go.
Where am I headed? I don't know yet.
But I'll get there first, on that you can bet.
I'm always competing, like I've been taught.
What will I win, what big fish can be caught?
We spend so much time just running the race
lost in our workload, taking up space.
We get lost in the shuffle, our daily routine.
Where is the value, can it be seen?
The winner of the rat race gets exactly what?
I don't know but I'll kick butt!
Is it better? Is it faster? Is it top of the line?
Do I look more cool than that friend of mine?
Can I keep up with old Smith and Jones?
Do I get more points working fingers to bones?
Who is the judge of this game anyway?
Do I get better results if I'm willing to pay?

They say confusion is the devil's best friend.
Can he keep you running after nothing until the end?
End life with the most toys and still you lose?
If you miss the light, if you miss the clues.
The Lord gave me life. What do I give back?
Am I even running on the right track?
I better search deeper, beyond the facade.
Exactly where in this world can I find God?
I'm making out something away from the race.
I start to see beauty. Could that be his face?
Away from the shuffle, away from the toys,
away from the fast cars, away from the noise.
The Lord can now find me. Don't it feel great!
All I had to do was unload my plate.
Ask for help to find your way
and you'll live on past judgment day.

IN THE ZONE

When game day comes we all want to win,
but are we deserving, did we put the time in?
The road is paved with work and sweat
and you won't be ready if you've not yet.
Put in the time and effort to build your skill.
It's so much more than just having the will.
Inspiration is such a curious thing,
the breath of life into some dead thing.
Man can move mountains if he's inspired.
With belief in a cause we can go way past tired.
When you truly believe in what you do
there is nothing on earth that can ever stop you.
Inspiration can come from thoughts divine,
or it can come when you've finally found your spine.
It can come in a dream or in broad daylight,
but when it comes, my friend, you'll have courage and might.
You'll have the burst of energy that we all need,
the extra shot through your body guaranteed
to be all they can handle and a little more.
No more knocking, you'll bust through the door
and say, "Hello world, here I am.
Look out for the lion that was a lamb."

When you trash-talk me, I say, “Game on.”
If you don’t bring some respect your chance is gone.
I can do this thing about which we talk.
I have no fear. I’m ready to rock.
I’ve worked and waited for this day
to hear my friends and family say,
“Never did I think he had the guts
to take some names and kick some butts.”
Never will they know the price you paid,
the hours you practiced, the foundation you laid,
the days you worked by yourself alone,
so that when it counted, *you were in the zone.*

MEANING OF LIFE

Where do you find the meaning of life?
Is it all summed up by two kids and a wife?

Do we have our life in the right sequence
with a two-story house and a white picket fence?

What is this wanderlust that I feel?
It's pulling hard and it seems so real.

There is something important that I must do.
Does that same feeling ever come over you?

All of life's distractions and still I need
something more on which to feed.

What unknown thing makes my head spin?
What causes bumps beneath my skin?

I can't pin it down, but still I know
there is somewhere else that I must go.

Where it is may not be clear
but I need to go and I have no fear.

I think I can lead, but I'm not sure
why I feel so calm and so secure.

For someone who doesn't know the way,
I feel strongly that I will someday.

I don't believe there's any text
to tell me what I must do next.

It comes down to feel, and what feels right
is to find that mountain, out of sight.

I can't see it yet, but I know it's there
and part of me will always be bare

until the day I stand atop
that hidden unicorn mountaintop.

The secrets of life I'll find that day.
And in the end, I knew the way.

DREAM BIG

Nothing approaches the power of a dream
no matter how long the odds might seem.

If you can dream it, you can do it
but that doesn't mean there's nothing to it.

God-given talent will only take you so far,
there are too many places to get stuck in the tar.

Some worthwhile goals take years to achieve
so if things don't happen fast, you still must believe.

Believe in yourself and the target you've set
but don't be discouraged if you're not there yet.

Mediocre people like to wallow in excuses.
You'll soon find they don't have many uses.

Go for your dream, even inches per step,
lift up those dreams rep after rep.

Do what you fear and fear will die.
You really won't know unless you try.

Time and effort can knock barriers down.
Leave fear behind and go to town.

The most important thing you own is your attitude.
Make sure that you're feeding it all the right food.

A man will never be worth more than his word
and success can fly away like a bird,

but a man who is loyal to what he has said
will find richness and value in the life he has led.

Dream big, my friends, and work hard, too.
Over time any dream can come to you.

PROBLEMS

Everyone has problems. That's really no excuse
to be mean and hateful or let your cannon loose.
What you say and do when the pressure is on
is how you'll be remembered long after you're gone.
'Cool under pressure' is really just a phrase
but it gains a whole new meaning when your life is ablaze.
How you treat others when your walls fall down
defines you as a person—or maybe as a clown.
Cellar dwellers will bring people down to where they are
but tearing others down won't make you a star.
You may say that it was done harmlessly in jest,
but don't your friends and family deserve your very best?
In everyone I've ever met, there's always been one thing
that you could praise about them that really wouldn't sting.
To live life with some baggage is what we have to do.
I can't imagine standing in someone else's shoe.
Instead, I'll think of something a little more divine
about the one who made the stars in heaven shine.
And if I can stop being so petty, don't you see,
maybe there will be a place up there for me.

YOU DON'T NEED FORTUNE

You don't need fortune, you don't need fame,
you don't need titles or letters before your name.
You just need God and His awesome word
to be in need of more now seems absurd.
You've been given some talents, you know that.
How can you use them? How can you step up and bat?
From point A to point B you don't need a map.
It seems you know how to cut through the crap.
If one word will do it, why use two?
Lets sift through the flour and find the clue.
The Lord gave His life for you and for me.
To ignore this fact would be a pity.
To think opinions or money are important at all
may lead to destruction, may cause our downfall.
Let's make our pursuits honest. Let's treat others well.
Don't let earthly trappings put us under a spell.
Because people are more important than time,
let's help each other. It isn't a crime.
So next time you can, let's do the right thing.
Down deep inside you the spirit will ring,
letting you know you've made the right choice.
Your life here does matter. You do have a voice.

MONEY

I'm going to talk to you all about your money.
Some of you won't think this is the least bit funny.

You will wonder out loud, "How could he dare?"
What is he thinking? Why does he care?

But don't you think that reaction is a little bit odd
when all of your blessings come from God?

What's yours is His, what's His is yours.
If you hold back His, will He hold back yours?

Are things just rosy and peachy and great?
Are things so good you just can't wait?

Maybe the reason things aren't going right,
maybe the reason your finances are tight

is because the Lord isn't first in the things you do.
Try putting Him in front of what you want for you.

Old Haggai told the people back when
they had to rebuild the Temple again.

The people needed to do the things he asked
or they would not prosper in any other task.

You can work hard in life to accumulate, I say,
and you'll still have nothing at the end of the day.

Because if you put God at the end of your list
some of the best things in life will surely be missed.

Your days could be filled with mishaps and strife
to remind you to put God first in your life.

And then like magic when you pass this test
amazingly your life may be blessed.

RETIREMENT

What happens to folks once they retire?
Is there nothing else to which they can aspire?
Is their experience not something that they can gift?
Is there no one's spirits that they can lift?
Must they hide out in a big fat camper,
leaving all life's work like dirty clothes in a hamper?
But you don't understand, this is what I deserved.
I worked all my life, now I want to be served.
I want to travel and see all this huge land.
I want to see the wonders of God's great hand.
I want to read and fish and go to the club,
and you better not tell me what to do, Bub.
I spent all my life just to get here,
now I'm going to relax, maybe have a tall beer.
I've got me some plans to eat drink and be merry,
don't want to work anymore. The thought's even scary.
But where in my plans did I put God?
As I look around this seems kind of odd.
Somewhere along the way, did I get off course?
As I think about it, I feel some remorse.
All my best laid plans just include me.
"There is nothing here for God," I say sheepishly.

O.K. All right. Maybe I'll reevaluate.
Maybe I can add a few things to my plate.
I could donate some time down at the shelter.
I could help a kid who's life is helter-skelter.
I was good at sports. I could be a coach.
There is really no subject that I couldn't broach.
I have many talents, and years left, few.
To find a way to heaven, there are many things I can do.
Now I realize I must waste no more time.
I could be here talking on my last dime.
As I finish this life, I must continue to give,
for if I do, forever I'll live.

DID YOU GIVE YOUR BEST TO GOD?

The question may sound a little odd,
but did you give your best to God?

On the computer today for a couple hours,
did you thank Him for His wonderful powers?

Watching T.V. until you fell asleep,
did you ask Him for your soul to keep?

On the way to work in traffic so thick,
did you say a prayer for those who are sick?

After you cashed your check down at the bank,
did you spend His share to fill your tank?

You're in God's sight as your chores you do.
When you don't need Him, He still needs you.

How can you go on days at a time
not speaking to Him just like a mime.

Living life in freedom, not paying your debt,
not giving credit for the gifts you get.

Would you be closer to Him today
if he took all sight and sound away?

In times of need do you pray and beg
when you think you're on life's last leg?

Is that the only time you do
what the Good Lord expects of you?

Do the Lord's work first and then your own
and your life will take a different tone.

Your work will be fruitless, your food will be bland
until you do the Lord's work and take His hand.

Mere mortal things won't light up your face
until you put God in His rightful place.

What seems important now will be forgotten.
Piles of worldly wealth will just seem rotten.

Only when all your excuses are gone,
only then, through Christ, can you live on.

SUNDAY NIGHT THUNDER

It’s Sunday night thunder. Let the music begin.
It’s Sunday night thunder, so settle on in.
Sit down and get comfy or stand up and shout.
Praise God in your own way. That’s what we’re about.
No special clothes and no special rules.
We’ll talk about Jesus and use different tools.
To raise your awareness and give you insight,
we’re taking the high road, seeking His light.
Climbing new mountains to see what we can see.
Taking you with us, be what you can be.
We’re going exploring, torch in our hand,
trekking His path to the promised land.
We’ll pray for His guidance. Join us please.
Don’t stay in the cold. We don’t want you to freeze.
And if you have something that you want to share,
come tell us about it. We really do care.
It’s Sunday night thunder, I’ll say it again.
It’s Sunday night thunder. Let the music begin.

FAITH

When I have faith I lose my worry.
Life calms down. I don't have to hurry.
When I have faith it doesn't matter
if the other guy brags about useless clatter.
When I have faith it seems real odd
to watch others chase things that don't include God.
So what is the moral of this story?
We have to work hard to spread God's glory.
Having something witty on your license plate
won't necessarily open heaven's gate.
Putting on fancy clothes with a new hairdo
won't do anything lasting for the inner you.
So let's give up pettiness. Don't try to be sly
and we might find a place in the sky.

THE FAR SIDE OF FEAR

Sometimes in life we falter;
sometimes in life we fail.
That doesn't mean we're nothing
dropped on the wrong side of the rail.

It's just time for some reflection,
gotta look hard in the mirror.
We gotta get ourselves acquainted
with the far side of our fear.

I met an old man walking
just the other day
I came upon him quickly
and he stepped out of my way.

There was something about his manner,
the way he smiled and tipped his cap.
I kept on moving forward,
then it hit me like a slap.

I had to get my questions answered,
put it in another gear,
because that old man was acquainted
with the far side of his fear.

Somehow I knew he had a story.
Somehow I knew I had to hear.
Somehow I knew there was a message,
what it was, was not yet clear.

Like a doctor he could heal me.
How I knew that, I don’t know,
but for a dollar’s worth of coffee
the old man helped me find my soul.

That old man had done some living.
“To hell and back,” is what he said.
But there’s just one thing that was giving him
that big smile that turned my head.

He said to forge the mighty river.
He said to climb the mountain high.
He said to slay the dragon demon.
Give faith in God a try.

BAD DATE

Timmy the Runt was a valuable kid.
We learned a lot from the nasty things he did.
One dark night at a football game
he gave more credence to his already bad name.
Off from the crowd he cornered a girl;
he and his buddies tried to give it a whirl.
The pretty brunette wouldn't give her consent,
but Timmy and his buddies just wouldn't relent.
They grabbed her and held her down for awhile.
Thank goodness someone came along and broke up the pile.
Timmy and his buddies got kicked out of school.
He blamed the poor girl like some kind of fool.
That girl and her reputation were never the same.
She has Timmy the Runt and his buddies to blame.
For the longest time she looked down when she walked
and she lost her beautiful smile whenever she talked.
She'd been assaulted, not raped, but the effect was clear,
to get her life back together took many a year.
Why didn't they understand that "no" means no?
Why did they have to push as far as they could go?
At least we can learn from the wrong others do,
then a few bad things don't have to happen to you.
Experience is one of our very best teachers.
You can learn a lot just sitting on the bleachers.

WARPED MINDS

The minds of the young can get warped these days.
They're exposed to evil in so many ways.
They've seen drugs and sex before they are teens.
It's hard telling how much crime they've seen.
Values and morals aren't shown much on T.V.
You must spend at least equal time to make kids see
indeed, there is a good side of life,
people can live happily as husband and wife.
The media bends over backwards to show the bad side of man.
It would be better to focus on good when we can.
To give kids a chance, we must parent well.
What dangers they'll face, we can't ever tell.
So whenever you can, spend time with a kid.
If you have a good family, that's what they did.
Teach them all that you know, help curb their mistakes,
help guide them along when their world shakes.
If you can raise them with just a small scratch or dent,
you might just help groom the next president.

DRUGS

Folks, let me tell you about the perils of drugs.
They put goofy looks on your pretty little mugs.

If somebody tells you on them you'll be cool,
I'd say you're hanging with some kind of fool.

Drugs make you dependent and mess up your life.
They'll kill you real slowly, not quick like a knife.

The first drugs are free from a supposed friend,
but then you'll be paying right up to the end.

Some kids try to see how high they can get.
They'll fly to the scene of the crash I would bet.

Whatever you try, the end result is bad,
and you'll lose the trust of your mom and your dad.

If they fool their parents, don't think they're sly.
Over dead children, all parents ask why.

"Why didn't we know? What were the signs?
Why couldn't we read between the lines?"

The bullies will tell you they can kick butts
and you're just a chicken without any guts.

But this is the time you need to be strong.
They'll get their feathers clipped before long.

Some will promise you happiness if you take a pill,
but the happy train always comes back *down* the hill

leaving you depressed, much worse than before,
pretty soon to be happy you'll have to score.

Some people claim drugs will do you no harm.
Be smart, don't let them twist on your arm.

Sometimes it's real easy to fit in with the crowd,
the ones headed nowhere and doing it real loud.

To hang there is easy. They just like to coast.
They have no ambition, brains fried like toast.

The answer is easy, "Just tell them No."
And there will be no limits on how far you can go.

COCAINE

There was a girl in town who was really "drop dead,"
gorgeous, that is, from her feet to her head.

She had the attention of all of the guys
and her star was really on the rise.

The potential she had was measured in tons.
She had brains to go with her cute little buns.

But then one day she was out with new friends
and she chose to go around one of life's little bends.

But up around the corner, what she couldn't see
was a path leading to trouble and misery.

You see, the path she chose was laced with cocaine
and it did something bad to the thoughts in her brain.

The goals in her life fell by the side
and before it let loose, her brain was fried.

She'd come to work and bounce off the walls
and finally her friends made one of those dreaded calls,

“You’ll have to come get her, she can’t work here.
She needs more help than we can give, I fear.”

But it seems the young girl wasn’t ready to quit.
“You people are crazy!” she said in a fit.

Her next little problem involved the law.
She was skin and bones and her senses were raw.

She broke into the house of a long-lost friend,
forced to steal because no one would lend.

She needed money, you see, to get her drug fix,
so she had to resort to unlawful tricks.

We hope it’s rock bottom, for that much we pray.
Her addiction will kill her if she can’t find her way.

If only potential guaranteed future success
she might be a model in a beautiful dress.

She made one bad choice on one bad day
and now she may never find her way.

ABORTION

Tell me what's up with this killing of babies
casting them out like lice or like scabies,
pretending I should have power of life or death,
pretending I should decide who takes a first breath.
Tell me why I should cancel somebody's life.
It wouldn't be handy, might cause too much strife?
Pretending it's O.K. to have freedom of choice,
that it's O.K to snuff out somebody's voice,
thinking it's just fine to mess with God's plan,
because we're so smart, we're the creature called man?
"Hey, it's my body, I'll do what I want.
I might be rich one day if I pull off this stunt."
"Children shouldn't have children," I've heard before.
But I was mature enough to open that door.
"I made a mistake. I rolled the dice,
but I'm too selfish, I won't pay the price."
Killing babies is arrogant and ill-conceived.
Do I really think I'll be relieved?
"Be quiet man, you're hitting a nerve."
If this is right, what God do I serve?
"If it's not breathing, it's not alive yet."
But you wouldn't trade places with *it,* I'll bet.

"Let's cut the crap. Let's put this to bed.
I know my child is not better off dead.
My life may be easier but filled with guilt.
Under self examination my motives just wilt.
Only through Jesus can I save my own life.
I'll have much to explain if I go under the knife.
I have to pop out of this self-absorbed mode
and pray for some help to lighten my load.
Killing my baby will never be right
and I may steer my own life out of God's sight.
Pray and think, and think and pray.
In the end I can answer only one way.
I must choose to give life, not put it out.
The golden rule is what it's about.
Embrace life's next corner. Go around the next bend.
God and family will be with me until the end."

BLESSED BE YOU, LITTLE MOTHER

Going from being a child to a wife—and then to a Mother
will be a journey unlike any other.

The wonder of carrying a child just beneath your heart
is like nothing else in life in which you will take part.

The first time you feel the baby move inside of you
makes you so happy you want to share it—and you do.

You call your husband at work to tell him all about it
and start thinking about all of the booties you will knit.

Changes in your body each month will be truly unique.
It isn't very long before you will not be able to see your feet.

Then comes the birth, the pain, the pushing and finally the rest.
And when they hand you your baby, you know you are truly blessed.

It is really something that we never remember the pain
because some of us do it time and time again.

—Marilyn Huisinga

WHAT MAKES WAR RIGHT?

Who's to say what makes war right?
Who's to say for what we should fight?
Mr. Bush would have America believe
he and his buddies did not deceive.
That good young soldiers do not toil
for greed and profit and simply oil.
Now they all scramble just to save face.
They say we had good cause to go to that place.
What is the value of one man's life?
Who will never again see his son or his wife?
Is this cause just? I do not know,
but I know I'm glad I don't have to go.
I want to be patriotic, but I have doubt
about the motives of the people who have the clout.
Terrorism is bad. America needs to be strong,
but something about this war seems very wrong.
"What would Jesus do?" I wonder out loud.
Is he mad? Is he happy? Is he proud?
I support our young soldiers, that's for sure,
but our reasons for being there need to be pure.

VOTE

I want to remind you of the last election, he wrote,
when some of you were too busy to vote.
I don't want to berate
but it wasn't just fate
that put our country in this unsteady boat.

Last time the course of our great country
was decided by a handful in Florida, you see.
They went to the polls
and punched out some holes
and gave us the president to be.

Whether he won by one, five, or ten,
you could say that the jury is definitely in.
So people don't cower.
Use your incredible power
and let's change the course of the world again.

Would our country's goals be the same
if more people had not been so lame?
Would we be at war
under Al Gore?
Would we be playing this terrorist game?

Sometimes for evil to exist
it just takes a few people to insist
my voice does not matter.
What nonsense they chatter.
Their man for president, goodbye they just kissed.

Yes it really was that close.
The thought is a little morose.
You should not have hurled
your chance to change the world,
then our situation would not be so gross.

So this time let me implore
that instead of stopping at the store
to pick up some beer
and have some good cheer
that you vote to help our country some more.

Real people who live anywhere
don't have to live in despair.
Stand up and be heard.
Register your word.
Show your country you really do care.

AM I THE HITLER OF MY TIME?

Verse 1
Am I the Hitler of my time?
Did I drop a bomb when I could've dropped a dime?
Can I stand before you here today
and say this war right here is the only way?
Can I say I'm not a prejudiced man
when I killed innocent people just like the clan?
How many people still have to die
now that we've caught the bad dictator guy?

Chorus
I say I'm the man and I'm always right
and you're not a patriot if you won't fight.
I say I'm the man. You better follow me
even if my motives you cannot see.
I say I'm the man. I say I'm the man.

Verse 2
Am I the leader of this world today?
Did I judge them fairly before I blew them away?
Will history be kind to me?
Did I consult the man from Galilee?
How many rules did I break
so I can justify the oil I take?
I'll put up a puppet to run that place
so I can win this election race.

Chorus
I say I'm the man and I'm always right.
And you're not a patriot if you won't fight.
I say I'm the man. I don't deceive.
Every word I say you better believe.
I say I'm the man. I say I'm the man.

Verse 3
Did I trade the cold war for this desert heat?
How many old mistakes did I repeat?
They've been fighting for over a thousand years.
I'll just settle things and have no fears.
I don't have an ego. I just have a plan
to solve their problems like only I can.
I'll make the world safe, just wait and see,
and you can give the Nobel Prize to me.

Chorus
I say I'm the man and I'm always right
and you're not a patriot if you won't fight.
I say I'm the man. You better follow me
even if my motives you cannot sec.
I say I'm the man. I say I'm the man.

DEATH IN IRAQ

We talk about justice and freedom and rights
but we must be ever so careful when we pick our fights
because in life there is little that stays absolute.
We can choose the wrong path if we get too cute.
There is black and there's white and between them is gray.
Where do we take our counsel when we choose our way?
Alas my friends, the Good Book is plain
we must not kill others. What have we to gain?
There are no exceptions. It always is wrong.
We can't make it right with a patriotic song.
Dropping bombs on the innocent folks in Iraq
has no lasting honor. It's a coward's attack.
Killing all in our way until we find the right one
has no justification. What in God's name have we done?
Whatever we've done, the Good Book is clear,
we will stand in judgment for what we've done here.
We may think all this blood can be washed from our hands
but these actions are timeless like ever-dropping sands.
These souls will haunt us until we change our ways.
They will always be with us as we live out our days.
There is but one way to make the world right again.
We must all stand up now and stop this great sin.

PERFECT

I wonder how long can Democracy last?
It seems it's fading—fading fast.
When powerful men can control the tribe
with the people's own money and a pork-barrel bribe?
When news channels report just what they want
and lead us to believe it's all up front?
When big money is protected to such a degree
that there's nothing left for you and for me?
When president "big shot" can go to war
and every night report the score?
"Got two of theirs, got three of mine."
Sounds like baseball with boxes of pine.
When monopoly is not a game?
When every gas price is exactly the same?
It sounds so wonderful. I'm filled with glee.
Yes, we have created the *perfect* democracy.

DIFFERENTISMS

We have phobias and "isms," each born of fear.
How quickly we notice you're not from around here.

We build chasms between us so far and wide,
let's think more like water and roll with the tide.

Saying this is what I am and this is what I ain't
is like looking at a wall with two shades of paint.

Which one is better? Which one more pure?
For this kind of thinking we must find a cure.

Everyone is different. Let's get that through our skull.
Why is it such a hard thing to mull?

We all have a blueprint. Each one unique.
Each individual person must find their own peak.

The reason you don't have someone else's tools
is your engine won't run on their blend of fuels.

The Lord gave us all a different personality.
We all have our gifts born from originality.

Why separate ourselves by race, color, creed?
When you have a cut, what color do you bleed?

I'm not like you, but can I be your friend?
When will we allow the stereotypes to end?

Let's get over the fear of different colors and sizes.
Let's work towards the day when everyone realizes

God put us all here, each with our own soul,
with a special ingredient, a piece of the whole.

To get rid of even one little slice of the pie
begs the question, "Why people, why?"

When we treat other people as if with God's own hand
that's when we'll conquer peace in this land.

RACISM

Racism is a thing I don't really understand,
when some people don't like it when blacks take a stand.
Why do people get judged by the color of their skin?
Just because you're white doesn't mean you're cool and fit in.
I thought the law said all people were created equally,
but accepting that fact does not seem to come easily.
Now, I'm a young lady and free from strife,
but some kids my age have been stabbed by a knife.
Looking different does not mean intentions are bad.
The way some people are treated really makes me sad.
I don't think people really think before they act
if they kill innocent people just because they're black.
One thing I do understand is that when I die, I hope it's not from
jealousy or hate.
I hope it is simply just my fate.

—Contributed by Ashley Huisinga

LET'S GET A CLUE

As I reread the books of the New Testament,
as I look at the reasons that Jesus was sent,
I haven't uncovered even one reason why
He would pick up a gun and kill another guy.
Do you think He would do it to protect His possessions?
Did He often resort to some sort of aggression?
Did He kill other men to protect promised land?
Did He get your respect by raising His hand?
Most generally, I found the answer was no,
the seeds of wisdom was what He would sow.
"Forgive them Lord, they know not what they do."
The moral majority must now get a clue.
Jesus came to die for all of our mistakes
as we give Him more to die for, my own heart aches.
When we send young people to die for who knows what,
I wonder how our minds got closed so shut.
We started out chasing Osama in Afghanistan
and end up in the desert chasing some other man.
We wanted revenge and found someone to pay.
This won't ever lead to our proudest day.
It's time to think and reign ourselves in.
Let's consult our Lord and be humble again.
In the Good Book we'll find just what we need
for the soul of our country I pray, Gods Speed.

TO MY CHILDREN

We never think it's urgent.
We think we'll always have a chance
to say the things we're thinking,
to give a loving glance.
My children mean the world to me.
I think they deserve to know
that if I'm not here tomorrow,
I'll always love them so.
My experiences so far in life
don't really make me smart,
but if I can share just some of them
my kids will have a good head start.
I won't be on earth forever,
of that I'm pretty sure,
but you need to know my love for you
will for eternity endure.
I won't take too many chances.
I'll try to live life right
so I can be around for you
and see your smiles so bright.
To share in your lives, always,
will be my fervent plan,
but if that doesn't happen,
I'll be your biggest fan.

So take life as it’s given.
Give the Lord your all.
Know He will always be there
even when you fall.
Sometimes in life things happen
we really can’t explain,
so if I can’t be here later
limping around with a cane,
you’ll know there were different plans
laid out in front of me.
I really can’t explain it,
just call it destiny.
You’ll have to make your own way
if you’ll be worth your salt
so if I can’t go with you,
let’s make it no ones fault.
Just thank God for the time we had
as a family together
and look to Him to help you through
all the stormy weather

—Love Dad